THE CORPORATE LANGUAGE

NAVIGATING THE TERMINOLOGY OF THE STARTUP WORLD

ROHAN SHAW

Made with ♥ on the Notion Press Platform
www.notionpress.com

Dedicated to all the dreamers, doers, and risk-takers who strive to make their mark on the world. May this book be a useful tool on your journey to create something meaningful and impactful. May it inspire you to reach new heights and achieve your entrepreneurial aspirations. To the startup community, thank you for your relentless pursuit of innovation and progress. This book is for you.

Contents

Contents

FOREWORD

Starting a business is one of the most challenging, yet rewarding, endeavors one can undertake. As an entrepreneur myself, I understand the importance of having a solid understanding of the key terms and concepts that shape the startup world. It is essential to have a strong foundation in the language of entrepreneurship to be able to navigate this complex and ever-evolving landscape.

That is why I am so grateful for "The Corporate Language: Navigating the Terminology of the Startup World" This guide provides a clear, concise, and accessible resource for anyone looking to understand the key terms used in the world of startups. From angel investors to bootstrapping, this book covers it all.

Whether you're a seasoned entrepreneur or just starting out, this book is an invaluable tool. It provides a reference point for all the key concepts and ideas that are essential to the startup world. Whether you're looking to expand your knowledge or simply need a quick reminder, "The Corporate Language" has got you covered.

I highly recommend this book to anyone who is looking to succeed in the world of startups. It is a must-have resource for any entrepreneur or aspiring entrepreneur. So dive in, and discover the essential terms and concepts that will help you succeed in the world of startups.

Rohan Shaw

FOREWORD

Starting a business is one of the most challenging, yet rewarding, endeavors one can undertake. As an entrepreneur myself, I understand the importance of having a solid understanding of the key terms and concepts that shape the startup world. It is essential to have a strong foundation in the language of entrepreneurship to be able to navigate this complex and ever-evolving landscape.

That is why I am so grateful for "The Corporate Language: Navigating the Terminology of the Startup World." This guide provides a clear, concise, and accessible resource for anyone looking to understand the key terms used in the world of startups. From angel investors to bootstrapping, this book covers it all.

Whether you're a seasoned entrepreneur or just starting out, this book is an invaluable tool. It provides a reference point for all the key concepts and ideas that are essential to the startup world. Whether you're looking [illegible]

[illegible] and also [illegible] the essential terms and concepts that will help you succeed in the world of startups.

[illegible]

Preface

The world of startups is filled with unique terms and concepts that can often be confusing and overwhelming. As a founder or investor, it is important to understand the language of business to succeed in the competitive world of startups. That's where "The Corporate Language: Navigating the Terminology of the Startup World" comes in.

This comprehensive guide provides a comprehensive overview of the key terms used in the startup world. From fundraising and valuation to product-market fit and exit terms, this book covers it all. With clear definitions, and explanations, you'll have the confidence to navigate the complex world of startups with ease.

Whether you're just starting out or looking to expand your knowledge, this book is an essential resource for anyone looking to succeed in the world of startups. So if you're ready to dive into the world of entrepreneurship, "The Corporate Language" is the perfect place to start.

Rohan Shaw

Preface

The world of startups is filled with unique terms and concepts that can often be confusing and overwhelming. As a founder or investor, it is important to understand the language of business to succeed in the competitive world of startups. That's where "The Corporate Language: Navigating the Terminology of the Startup World" comes in.

This comprehensive guide provides a comprehensive overview of the key terms used in the startup world. From fundraising and valuation to product-market fit and exit terms, this book covers it all. With clear definitions and explanations, you'll have the confidence to navigate the complex world of startups with ease.

Whether you're just starting out or looking to expand your knowledge, this book is an essential resource for anyone looking to succeed in the world of startups. So if you're ready to dive into the world of entrepreneurship, [illegible] is the perfect place to start.

[illegible]

Acknowledgements

Writing this book would not have been possible without the support and guidance of many individuals. I would like to take this opportunity to extend my sincerest gratitude to the following people:

First and foremost, I would like to thank my family for their unwavering support and encouragement. Their love and belief in me has been a constant source of inspiration throughout this journey.

I would also like to thank my colleagues and peers in the startup world who have shared their experiences and insights with me. Your contributions have been invaluable in shaping the content of this book.

Lastly, I would like to express my appreciation to all the readers of this book. I hope that this guide proves to be a valuable resource in your journey to succeed in the world of startups.

Rohan Shaw

PROLOGUE

The world of startups is a constantly evolving landscape, filled with new ideas, technologies, and innovations. To succeed in this dynamic environment, it is essential to have a strong understanding of the key terms and concepts that shape the startup world.

In this book, "The Corporate Language: Navigating the Terminology of the Startup World," we will explore the most important terms used in the world of startups. From fundraising and valuation to product-market fit and exit terms, this comprehensive guide will provide you with a deep understanding of the language of business.

Whether you're just starting out or looking to expand your knowledge, this book is the perfect resource for anyone looking to succeed in the world of startups. So if you're ready to dive into the exciting world of entrepreneurship, turn the page and discover the essential terms that will help you navigate the startup world with confidence.

Rohan Shaw

A

Angel investor: An individual who provides capital to startups in exchange for equity or convertible debt.

Acquisition: The process of acquiring another company or its assets to grow and expand the business.

Agile methodology: A project management approach that emphasizes flexibility and adaptability, allowing teams to respond quickly to changes and customer needs.

Alpha testing: The first stage of software testing, where the product is tested by a select group of users before it is released to the public.

API (Application Programming Interface): A set of protocols and routines for building software applications that allow different software systems to communicate and exchange data.

Asset: Anything of value owned by a company, including physical assets (such as equipment) and intangible assets (such as patents).

AT&T Park: A popular term used to describe the home field of the San Francisco Giants baseball team.

Attrition rate: The rate at which employees leave a company, typically due to retirement, resignation, or termination.

Augmented reality (AR): A technology that enhances reality by overlaying digital information on the physical world.

Automation: The use of technology to automate manual tasks and processes, allowing companies to improve efficiency and reduce costs.

A/B testing: A method of testing where two variations of a product or campaign are compared to determine which is more effective.

Accounting: The process of recording, classifying, and summarizing financial transactions to provide information that is useful for decision making.

Acquisition cost: The cost of acquiring an asset, including the purchase price and any related expenses.

Acquisition integration: The process of integrating the operations and processes of two companies after an acquisition.

Acquisition strategy: A plan for acquiring other companies or assets in order to grow and expand the business.

Advertising: The promotion of a product or service through various media, such as print, television, or digital advertising.

Advisory board: A group of individuals who provide advice and guidance to a company or startup on strategic, operational, and other important matters.

Affiliate marketing: A performance-based marketing strategy where affiliates are paid a commission for promoting a company's products or services.

Angel round: A funding round in which a startup raises capital from angel investors.

Anti-dilution provision: A clause in a stock purchase agreement that protects investors from dilution of their ownership stake in the event of future equity financing rounds.

App store: A digital platform where users can browse, download, and purchase mobile applications.

Application: A software program designed to perform a specific task or set of tasks.

Arrears: A term used to describe a debt that is overdue or has not been paid on time.

Article of incorporation: A legal document that is filed with a government agency to form a corporation.

Assets under management (AUM): A metric used to measure the total value of assets that are managed by an investment firm.

Audit: A systematic examination of a company's financial records and operations to determine compliance with laws and regulations and to identify potential risks.

Authenticity: The degree to which a product or service is true to its original purpose or design.

Autonomous vehicle: A vehicle that is capable of operating without human input or supervision.

Available cash: The amount of cash that is readily available for use, taking into account any outstanding debts or obligations.

Average revenue per user (ARPU): A metric used to measure the average revenue generated from each user of a product or service.

Awards and recognition: A program or initiative that acknowledges and rewards employees for their contributions and achievements.

Awareness: The extent to which consumers are aware of a product, service, or brand.

Active listening: A communication technique in which the listener fully focuses on, understands, and reflects upon what is being said.

Alpha release: An early version of a product or software released to a select group of users for testing and feedback, prior to a full release.

Application software: Software designed to perform specific tasks, such as word processing, accounting, or project management.

Artificial intelligence (AI): The development of computer systems that can perform tasks that typically require human intelligence, such as visual perception, speech recognition, and decision-making.

Audience segmentation: The process of dividing a market into smaller groups based on characteristics such as age, gender, or behavior, allowing for targeted marketing efforts.

Autonomous technology: Technology that operates independently, without the need for direct human control or intervention.

B

Backlog: A list of tasks or projects that are waiting to be completed.

Balance sheet: A financial statement that provides a snapshot of a company's financial position, including its assets, liabilities, and equity.

Bandwidth: A measure of the amount of data that can be transmitted over a network in a given amount of time.

Bank financing: A type of financing where a company borrows money from a bank to fund its operations or growth.

Bankruptcy: A legal process where a company is unable to pay its debts and seeks protection from its creditors.

Bartering: An exchange of goods or services between two parties without the exchange of money.

Behavioral targeting: A type of targeted advertising that is based on a consumer's online behavior, such as web browsing history or search terms.

Beta testing: The second stage of software testing, where the product is tested by a wider group of users before it is released to the public.

Bill of materials (BOM): A list of all the raw materials, components, and subassemblies required to manufacture a product.

Black swan event: An unexpected and high-impact event that has a significant impact on a business or industry.

Blog: A website or platform where an individual or organization can publish regular posts, articles, and other content.

Blue-sky thinking: A type of creative thinking that encourages exploring new ideas and possibilities without being limited by constraints or assumptions.

Board of directors: A group of individuals who are elected by a company's shareholders to oversee its management and operations.

Bootstrapping: A type of startup financing where a founder uses personal savings, loans, and other means to fund their company without outside investment.

Bottom-up approach: An approach to decision making where decisions are made based on individual components or details, rather than overall goals or objectives.

Brainstorming: A creative problem-solving technique where a group of individuals share ideas and suggestions to find a solution to a problem.

Break-even point: The point at which a company's revenue is equal to its expenses, resulting in neither a profit nor a loss.

Bridge financing: A type of short-term financing that provides interim funding until a company is able to secure a more permanent source of funding.

Build, measure, learn: A process used in Lean Startup methodologies, where a company builds a minimum viable product, measures its performance, and uses the data to learn and make improvements.

Business angel: A wealthy individual who provides financial and mentorship support to startups in exchange for equity or a share of the company's profits.

Business incubator: A program or facility that provides support and resources to early-stage startups, including office space, mentorship, and networking opportunities.

Business model: A plan or strategy for how a company will generate revenue and profit.

Business plan: A formal written document that outlines a company's strategy, including its goals, target market, marketing and sales plans, and financial projections.

Business-to-business (B2B): A type of business relationship where a company sells its products or services to another company.

Business-to-consumer (B2C): A type of business relationship where a company sells its products or services directly to consumers.

Buyout: A type of acquisition where one company purchases all of the outstanding shares of another company.

By-laws: A set of rules and regulations that govern the internal affairs of a corporation or organization.

Buyer persona: A fictional representation of a company's ideal customer, based on market research and data analysis.

Backend development: The development of the server-side components of a software application, responsible for storing and processing data.

Beta release: A pre-release version of a product or software that is made available to a wider group of users for testing and feedback.

Big data: Large, complex data sets that are difficult to process and analyze using traditional methods, requiring advanced technologies and techniques to extract insights and value.

Blockchain: A decentralized, distributed ledger technology that records transactions across a network of computers, ensuring the integrity and transparency of data.

Branding: The process of creating and establishing a unique identity for a company or product, through elements such as name, logo, and marketing materials.

Break-even analysis: A calculation of the point at which a business's revenue matches its expenses, indicating when it will start to make a profit.

Burn rate: The rate at which a company is using up its cash reserves.

Business analyst: A professional who helps organizations improve their processes and systems, by gathering and analyzing data, identifying problems, and recommending solutions.

Business continuity: The planning and preparation for unexpected events that could disrupt normal business operations, including natural disasters, power outages, and cyber attacks.

Business model: The way a company creates, delivers, and captures value, by combining its resources and capabilities to meet the needs of its customers and generate revenue.

Business process outsourcing (BPO): The practice of outsourcing certain business processes, such as payroll or customer service, to external providers.

C

Capital: Money or other assets that a company can use to fund its operations, growth, and investments.

Capital expenditures: Money that a company spends on long-term investments, such as equipment, property, and infrastructure.

Capitalization: The total value of a company's outstanding stock and outstanding debt.

Cash flow: The movement of money into and out of a company, including its revenues, expenses, and investments.

Channel distribution: The process of distributing a company's products or services through intermediaries, such as wholesalers, retailers, or distributors.

Collaboration: The process of working together with others to achieve a common goal.

Collective bargaining: The negotiation process between a union and an employer to reach an agreement on working conditions and wages.

Competitor analysis: The process of researching and evaluating a company's competitors and their products, services, and market position.

Competitive advantage: A factor or combination of factors that sets a company apart from its competitors and gives it a better position in the market.

Competitive intelligence: Information and insights about a company's competitors, including their strategies, products, and market performance.

Complex sale: A sales process that involves multiple decision-makers, a lengthy decision-making process, and multiple stages of negotiation.

Compliance: Adhering to laws, regulations, and standards that apply to a company or industry.

Concentric diversification: A strategy of expanding a company's operations by adding new products or services that are related to its core business.

Concept stage: The initial stage of a startup, where an idea for a new product or service is developed and refined.

Configuration management: The process of managing changes to a product or system throughout its lifecycle, including its design, development, and production.

Conglomerate: A company that consists of multiple businesses or subsidiaries operating in different industries.

Consumer goods: Products that are manufactured and sold directly to consumers, such as food, clothing, and household items.

Consumer packaged goods (CPG): Products that are sold in retail stores and are consumed by end-users, such as food, drinks, and personal care items.

Consumer research: The process of collecting and analyzing data about consumer behavior, preferences, and attitudes to inform marketing and sales strategies.

Consumer-to-consumer (C2C): A type of business relationship where consumers sell products or services directly to other consumers, such as through online marketplaces.

Complex sale: A sales process that involves multiple decision-makers, a lengthy decision-making process, and multiple stages of negotiation.

Compliance: Adhering to laws, regulations, and standards that apply to a company or industry.

Concentric diversification: A strategy of expanding a company's operations by adding new products or services that are related to its core business.

Concept stage: The initial stage of a startup, where an idea for a new product or service is developed and refined.

Configuration management: The process of managing changes to a product or system throughout its lifecycle, including its design, development, and production.

Conglomerate: A company that consists of multiple businesses or subsidiaries operating in different industries.

Consumer goods: Products that are manufactured and sold directly to consumers, such as food, clothing, and household items.

Consumer packaged goods (CPG): Products that are sold in retail stores and are consumed by end-users, such as food, drinks, and personal care items.

Consumer research: The process of collecting and analyzing data about consumer behavior, preferences, and attitudes to inform marketing and sales strategies.

Consumer-to-consumer (C2C): A type of business relationship where consumers sell products or services directly to other consumers, such as through online marketplaces.

Customer Acquisition Cost (CAC): The cost of acquiring a new customer, including marketing, sales, and customer support expenses.

Customer Lifetime Value (CLV): The estimated value that a customer will bring to a company over the course of their relationship.

Customer relationship management (CRM): The process of managing interactions with customers and clients, including sales, marketing, and customer support.

Customer satisfaction: The degree to which a customer is satisfied with a company's products or services.

Customer Segmentation: The process of dividing a customer base into smaller groups based on common characteristics, such as demographics, behavior, or psychographics.

Customer Service: The support provided to customers before, during, and after a sale, including technical support, product information, and problem resolution.

Cybersecurity: The protection of information and systems from unauthorized access, use, disclosure, disruption, modification, or destruction.

Capital expenditure (CapEx): Money spent by a company on long-term assets, such as property, plant, and equipment, that are expected to provide value over multiple years.

Channel partner: A company or individual that promotes and sells the products or services of another company, typically in exchange for a commission or fee.

Chief Executive Officer (CEO): The highest-ranking executive in a company, responsible for overall strategy and performance.

Chief Financial Officer (CFO): The executive responsible for a company's financial operations, including accounting, budgeting, and financial reporting.

Chief Operating Officer (COO): The executive responsible for the day-to-day operations of a company, including overseeing production and delivery of goods or services.

Chief Marketing Officer (CMO): The executive responsible for a company's marketing strategy, including advertising, public relations, and product development.

Chief Technology Officer (CTO): The executive responsible for a company's technology strategy, including research and development, information systems, and cybersecurity.

Chief Information Officer (CIO): The executive responsible for a company's information technology strategy, including data management, software development, and hardware systems.

Chief Human Resources Officer (CHRO): The executive responsible for a company's human resources strategy, including employee relations, recruitment, and benefits.

Chief Legal Officer (CLO): The executive responsible for a company's legal strategy, including risk management, contracts, and compliance.

Chief Supply Chain Officer (CSCO): The executive responsible for a company's supply chain strategy, including procurement, logistics, and distribution.

Chief Business Development Officer (CBDO): The executive responsible for a company's business development strategy, including partnerships, acquisitions, and growth initiatives.

Cloud computing: The delivery of computing resources and services, such as storage, processing, and software, over the internet, on an as-needed basis.

Code review: The process of examining and evaluating code written by another developer, to ensure that it meets quality and standards requirements.

Collaboration software: Software tools that enable teams to work together on projects and tasks, by providing features such as task management, file sharing, and real-time communication.

Commission: A fee or payment based on the performance of a salesperson or partner, calculated as a percentage of the revenue generated by their sales.

Conversion rate optimization (CRO): The process of improving the conversion rate of a website or business, by analyzing data and testing changes to the user experience.

Corporate strategy: The plan and approach that a company uses to compete and succeed in its market, including decisions on products, markets, and organizational structure.

D

Data analysis: The process of collecting, cleaning, and analyzing data to draw insights and inform business decisions.

Data privacy: The protection of personal information and other sensitive data from unauthorized access, use, or disclosure.

Debt financing: The process of raising capital by borrowing money, either from banks, other lenders, or investors.

Debt-to-equity ratio: A financial ratio that measures a company's debt relative to its equity, which reflects the extent to which it relies on debt financing.

Delegation: The act of assigning responsibility and authority to others to complete a task or manage a project.

Delivery: The process of transporting goods or services to customers, including the planning, execution, and management of logistics.

Demand generation: The process of creating interest and awareness of a product or service among potential customers.

Demand planning: The process of forecasting future demand for a product or service, taking into account market trends, consumer behavior, and other factors.

Departmentalization: The process of organizing a company into distinct units or departments based on function, geography, product, or customer.

Depreciation: The decline in the value of an asset over time, typically due to wear and tear, obsolescence, or changes in the market.

Design thinking: An approach to problem-solving that emphasizes empathy, experimentation, and iteration, and seeks to understand the needs of users and create solutions that meet those needs.

Development stage: The stage of a startup's lifecycle when the product or service is being developed and tested.

Digital marketing: The use of digital channels and technologies, such as social media, email, search engines, and mobile devices, to promote and sell products or services.

Direct mail: A marketing technique that involves sending promotional materials directly to potential customers, either through the mail or by email.

Direct marketing: A marketing approach that seeks to reach potential customers directly, bypassing intermediaries such as retailers or wholesalers.

Diversity and inclusion: The recognition and appreciation of differences in people, including differences in race, gender, ethnicity, sexual orientation, and other personal characteristics, and the promotion of a workplace culture that values and respects these differences.

Diversification: The process of spreading investment risk by investing in a range of different assets, industries, or geographic regions.

Due diligence: The process of thoroughly investigating and evaluating a business, investment opportunity, or other potential acquisition before making a final decision.

Demographic: A statistical category that describes a population based on characteristics such as age, gender, race, income, and education.

Deployment: The process of releasing and distributing software or other products to users or customers.

Distribution channel: The path or route through which a product or service reaches the end customer, including wholesalers, retailers, and online platforms.

E

Earnings before interest, taxes, depreciation, and amortization (EBITDA): A measure of a company's financial performance that excludes interest, taxes, depreciation, and amortization expenses.

Economic order quantity (EOQ): A mathematical formula used to determine the optimal order quantity for inventory, taking into account the trade-off between the cost of carrying inventory and the cost of placing orders.

Employee engagement: The degree to which employees feel connected to, satisfied with, and committed to their job and the company.

Employee retention: The ability of a company to retain its employees over time, measured by the rate at which employees leave the company.

Employment tracking: The process of monitoring the progress of a project or task, typically by tracking milestones, deadlines, and other key indicators.

Equity financing: The process of raising capital by issuing shares of stock or ownership in the company, either to investors or the public.

Equity multiple: A financial metric that measures the multiple of investment returns relative to the original investment, used to evaluate the performance of a private equity investment.

Exit strategy: The plan for a business owner or investor to sell or transfer ownership of their stake in a company.

Expense management: The process of controlling and reducing a company's expenses, including cost-saving measures and budgeting.

Export: The sale of goods or services to customers outside of a company's home market.

External audit: An independent assessment of a company's financial records and practices, typically performed by a third-party accounting firm.

External environment: The factors and forces outside of a company that can impact its performance, including economic conditions, competition, regulation, and technology.

External stakeholder: A person, group, or organization that has a vested interest in the performance or actions of a company, but is not directly involved in its operations.

Extreme value analysis: A statistical analysis that seeks to identify outliers or extreme values in data, which may indicate trends, anomalies, or errors.

Eyeball test: An informal evaluation or assessment of a product or service, based on personal observation or intuition.

Employee stock ownership plan (ESOP): A type of retirement plan that invests in the stock of the employer company.

Entrepreneur: A person who starts and manages a new business, typically taking on financial risks in pursuit of profits.

F

Fair market value: The estimated price that a willing buyer and seller would agree on, taking into account current market conditions and the characteristics of the property being sold.

Family office: A private wealth management firm that serves a single wealthy family, providing investment management, tax planning, estate planning, and other financial services.

Feasibility study: An evaluation of the potential success of a proposed project or business, based on market research, financial analysis, and other relevant data.

Financial advisor: A professional who provides advice and guidance on financial matters, such as investment planning, retirement planning, tax planning, and risk management.

Financial analysis: The process of evaluating a company's financial performance and condition, typically using financial ratios, trend analysis, and other tools.

Financial leverage: The use of borrowed money or other forms of debt to increase the potential return on investment, by amplifying the impact of positive performance.

Financial planning: The process of creating a comprehensive plan for managing one's finances, including setting financial goals, creating a budget, and investing for the future.

Financial ratio: A numerical comparison of two or more financial metrics, used to evaluate a company's financial performance and condition.

Financial reporting: The process of providing information about a company's financial performance and condition to stakeholders, through financial statements and other disclosures.

Financial risk: The potential for loss or damage to a company's financial position, due to a variety of factors such as market volatility, interest rate fluctuations, or currency fluctuations.

First-mover advantage: The competitive advantage that a company gains by being the first to enter a new market or to introduce a new product or service.

First-to-market: The first company to introduce a new product or service in a particular market.

Flat organization: A management structure that has few or no levels of hierarchy, resulting in a more decentralized and democratic decision-making process.

Flexible work arrangements: Work arrangements that allow employees to have some degree of control over when, where, and how they work, such as telecommuting, part-time work, and flexible schedules.

Fractional ownership: A type of ownership in which multiple individuals own a portion of a property or asset, typically used for high-value assets such as private jets, yachts, or vacation homes.

Franchise: A business model in which a franchisor grants a franchisee the right to operate a business using the franchisor's trademark, products, and business systems.

Freelance worker: A self-employed individual who offers their services to clients on a project-by-project basis, rather than as a full-time employee.

Full-service marketing: A type of marketing that provides a comprehensive range of services, including market research, product development, advertising, public relations, and sales.

Funding round: A stage in a company's financing cycle in which it raises capital from investors, typically through the issuance of equity or debt securities.

Futures contract: A legally binding agreement between two parties to buy or sell a specified asset at a predetermined price on a specified future date.

Financial projections: Estimates of a company's future financial performance, based on assumptions about revenue, expenses, and growth.

Focus group: A small, selected group of individuals who are brought together to provide feedback on a product, service, or marketing campaign.

Foreign direct investment (FDI): Investments made by a company or individual in a foreign country, such as by acquiring a foreign company or setting up operations abroad.

G

GAAP (Generally Accepted Accounting Principles): A set of guidelines and rules for financial reporting, used by companies in the United States to ensure consistency and transparency in their financial statements.

Growth hacking: A data-driven approach to marketing and product development, aimed at maximizing a company's growth potential.

Growth stage: The stage in a company's life cycle when it is focused on expanding its operations, increasing market share, and becoming profitable.

Gross Margin: The difference between a company's revenue and cost of goods sold, expressed as a percentage of revenue.

Greenfield Investment: A type of investment in a new or undeveloped market, typically involving the construction of new facilities and infrastructure.

Globalization: The process of increasing interconnectedness and interdependence between countries and businesses, through the exchange of goods, services, and information.

Go-to-Market (GTM) strategy: A plan for bringing a product or service to market, including market segmentation, target customers, pricing, and marketing channels.

Gross Domestic Product (GDP): A measure of a country's economic output, equal to the total value of all goods and services produced within its borders in a given time period.

Government procurement: The process by which government agencies purchase goods and services from private sector suppliers.

Gross Profit: The total revenue of a company, minus the cost of goods sold.

General Partner (GP): The managing partner in a partnership, who is responsible for overseeing the day-to-day operations of the business.

Goodwill: An intangible asset that represents the value of a company's reputation, customer base, and other intangible assets that are not easily quantifiable.

Guaranteed Issue: A type of insurance policy that is offered without regard to the individual's health or medical history.

Gross Lease: A type of lease agreement in which the tenant pays a single, fixed rent that covers all operating expenses, including property taxes and maintenance costs.

Growth Equity: A type of private equity investment that provides capital to growing companies, typically in exchange for a minority stake in the business.

Geolocation: The process of determining the geographic location of a device or user, typically through the use of GPS or other technologies.

Global Supply Chain: A network of suppliers, manufacturers, distributors, and retailers that spans multiple countries and continents, and is responsible for the production and delivery of goods and services to customers around the world.

Government grants: Financial assistance provided by a government to support specific activities, such as research and development or business expansion.

Gross revenue: The total amount of money a company generates from the sale of goods or services, before any expenses are deducted.

Globalization Index: A measure of the degree to which countries and businesses are integrated into the global economy, based on factors such as trade, investment, and migration.

Green Energy: Energy generated from renewable sources, such as wind, solar, hydro, and biomass, that are considered to be environmentally friendly and sustainable.

Global Marketing: The process of creating and executing marketing strategies that reach customers and markets across multiple countries and continents.

H

Hedge fund: An investment fund that uses a variety of strategies to generate returns, including long and short positions in equities, commodities, currencies, and other assets.

High-net-worth individual (HNWI): An individual with a net worth of $1 million or more, excluding their primary residence.

Holding company: A company that owns and manages other companies, typically as a means of diversifying its business and reducing risk.

Human resources (HR): The department within a company responsible for recruiting, training, and managing employees, as well as overseeing employee benefits and compensation programs.

Hyper-local: Refers to a marketing strategy that targets customers in a specific geographic location, often at a very granular level, such as a neighborhood or street.

Harvest strategy: A plan for how a venture capital firm will eventually exit its investments and realize returns, such as by selling its stake to another investor or taking the company public.

Human Capital: The knowledge, skills, and experience of a company's employees, considered as a valuable asset that contributes to the success of the business.

High-Growth Startup: A startup company that is growing rapidly, often characterized by high levels of revenue and user acquisition.

Horizontal Integration: The process of acquiring or merging with companies in the same industry or product line, in order to expand a company's market share and increase efficiency.

Hybrid Model: A business model that combines elements of different business models, such as combining e-commerce and brick-and-mortar retail.

Hosting Services: Services that provide computer storage and access to the Internet for websites, applications, and other online content.

House Account: An account established by a company for the purpose of conducting business with another company or individual.

Hard Money Loan: A type of loan that is secured by real property, typically used for short-term, high-interest financing, such as for real estate investments.

Handshake Deal: An informal agreement made between two parties, without a written contract.

Headcount: The number of employees in a company or organization.

Health Savings Account (HSA): A type of savings account that is specifically designed for individuals with high-deductible health insurance plans, offering tax-advantaged savings on medical expenses.

Heavy User: A customer who uses a product or service frequently, often to an extent that exceeds the average usage patterns of other customers.

Holdout Problem: The challenge of getting all parties involved in a negotiation to agree on the same terms, especially when some parties are reluctant to compromise.

Holding Company: A company that owns and controls other companies, often with the goal of centralizing management and increasing economies of scale.

Human Resource Management (HRM): The process of managing a company's employees, including hiring, training, compensation, and benefits administration.

Human Resource Planning (HRP): The process of identifying and anticipating the future needs of a company's workforce, in order to ensure that the right number and mix of employees are available at the right time.

High-Performance Team: A team of employees that consistently delivers exceptional results, often due to factors such as clear goals, strong communication, and mutual trust and respect.

Human Resource Information System (HRIS): A software application that provides automated support for various aspects of human resource management, such as payroll processing and benefits administration.

Hypothesis Testing: The process of using data and statistical analysis to test a theory or assumption, often in order to determine whether it is supported by the evidence or not.

Historical Cost Accounting: An accounting method that values assets and liabilities at their original cost, regardless of any changes in market value that may have occurred since then.

Horizon Scanning: The process of identifying and assessing emerging trends, technologies, and other factors that are likely to have an impact on a company or industry in the future.

Hurdle Rate: The minimum rate of return that a company or investment must achieve in order for it to be considered successful.

Hard Cap: The maximum amount of funding that a company is seeking to raise through a crowdfunding campaign or other fundraising effort.

Heart of the Business: The core activities, processes, and functions that are critical to a company's success, and that are often the main focus of management attention and investment.

Human Factors Engineering: The application of engineering and design principles to the development of products and services that are well-suited to the physical and cognitive capabilities of human users.

I

Idea Generation: The process of coming up with new and innovative ideas for products, services, or business models.

Intellectual Property (IP): A category of property that includes patents, trademarks, copyrights, trade secrets, and other legally-protected forms of intangible assets.

Incubator: A program or organization that provides resources, mentorship, and other support to help early-stage startups grow and develop.

Initial Coin Offering (ICO): A type of crowdfunding campaign that uses blockchain technology and digital tokens to raise funds for a new cryptocurrency or blockchain-based project.

Initial Public Offering (IPO): The process of taking a privately-held company public by issuing shares of stock to the public, often in order to raise capital.

Innovation: The introduction of new ideas, products, services, or business models that can create value and differentiate a company from its competitors.

Institutional Investor: A large financial institution, such as a bank, pension fund, or hedge fund, that invests capital on behalf of its clients or members.

Insurtech: A term used to describe the application of technology and innovation to the insurance industry, often with the goal of improving the efficiency and customer experience of insurance products and services.

Integrative Thinking: A problem-solving approach that involves considering multiple perspectives, breaking down silos, and synthesizing new solutions from disparate parts.

Intellectual Capital: The knowledge, skills, and experience of a company's employees, often seen as a valuable asset that can be leveraged to create competitive advantage.

Internal Rate of Return (IRR): A financial metric used to evaluate the potential profitability of an investment, by comparing the estimated returns to the costs of the investment.

Intrapreneurship: The process of fostering a culture of entrepreneurship and innovation within a larger company, often by encouraging employees to identify and pursue new opportunities for growth and development.

Investor: A person or entity who provides funding to a startup or business in exchange for ownership equity or debt.

Iteration: A repetition of a process in order to improve or refine a product or service.

Initial Seed Funding: The first round of financing for a startup, usually from friends, family, and angel investors.

Investor Pitch: A presentation given by a founder to potential investors, highlighting the company's product, market, and growth potential.

Investment Banker: A financial professional who assists companies in raising capital through securities offerings and other financial transactions.

Investor Relations: The practice of managing communication between a company and its investors, including the dissemination of financial information and investor updates.

Inventory Management: The process of overseeing and controlling the flow of goods and materials in a company's supply chain.

J

Joint Venture: A strategic alliance between two or more companies to pursue a common business goal.

Job Description: A document that outlines the duties, responsibilities, and qualifications required for a specific job position.

J-Curve: A graphical representation of the typical cash flow pattern of a private equity investment, showing negative cash flow in the early years followed by positive cash flow in later years.

Joint Stock Company: A type of business organization where ownership is divided into shares of stock, which can be bought and sold by shareholders.

Jumpstart Our Business Startups (JOBS) Act: A US federal law enacted in 2012 that eases restrictions on private companies seeking to go public.

Just-In-Time (JIT) Inventory: An inventory management system where items are ordered and received only as they are needed for production, reducing the need for large amounts of storage space and reducing waste.

Junior Bond: A bond with a lower credit rating and higher interest rate compared to senior bonds issued by the same company.

Junior Equity: Equity ownership in a company that has lower priority than senior equity in terms of claim on assets and earnings.

K

Key Performance Indicator (KPI): A metric used to evaluate the success of an organization or specific aspect of its operations in achieving its objectives.

Key Man Insurance: A type of insurance policy that compensates a company for financial loss if a key employee dies or becomes disabled.

Kickstart: A process of jumpstarting a stalled or underperforming business by implementing changes in strategy, operations, or management.

Knowledge Management: The process of creating, sharing, using, and managing the knowledge and information of an organization.

Knockout Option: A type of option contract that becomes null and void if the underlying asset reaches a certain price level.

L

Leverage: The use of borrowed money to increase the potential return of an investment.

Liquidity: The ability of an asset to be easily converted into cash without affecting its price.

Limited Liability Company (LLC): A type of business structure that combines the liability protection of a corporation with the tax benefits of a partnership.

Long-Term Debt: Debt that is due more than one year in the future.

Loss Leader: A product that is sold at a price lower than its cost, with the aim of attracting customers and generating profits through other sales.

Lead Generation: The process of finding and cultivating potential customers for a business's products or services.

Lean Startup: A business methodology that emphasizes rapid iteration, continuous testing and improvement, and efficient use of resources.

Letter of Intent (LOI): A non-binding document outlining the preliminary terms and conditions of a proposed business transaction.

Licensing Agreement: A legal agreement between a licensor and a licensee that grants the latter the right to use the licensor's intellectual property in exchange for royalties or other compensation.

Line of Credit: An agreement between a lender and a borrower that allows the borrower to access funds up to a specified limit as needed.

M

Market capitalization: The total value of a company's outstanding shares of stock, calculated as the number of shares times the price per share.

Market research: The process of gathering and analyzing information about target markets and customers, to inform marketing and business strategy.

Marketing mix: The elements of a company's marketing strategy, including product, price, place, and promotion.

Merger: The combination of two or more companies into a single entity, typically for the purpose of achieving synergies, expanding market reach, or increasing market share.

Mission statement: A concise statement that defines a company's purpose, values, and priorities, and guides its decision-making and actions.

Monetization: The process of converting a product, service, or technology into a revenue-generating opportunity.

Motivation: The forces that drive an individual or organization to act in a certain way, such as incentives, rewards, or a sense of purpose.

Marketing automation: The use of software to automate repetitive marketing tasks, such as email campaigns and lead nurturing.

Minimum viable product (MVP): The minimum set of features needed to launch a product or service and start learning from early adopters.

Mobile app: A software application designed to run on mobile devices, such as smartphones and tablets.

Monetization: The process of converting a product, service, or user base into revenue.

N

Network Effect: The phenomenon where the value of a product or service increases as more people use it.

Niche Market: A narrowly defined segment of the market for a specific product or service.

Non-Disclosure Agreement (NDA): A legally binding agreement that restricts the sharing of confidential information.

Non-compete Agreement: A legal agreement between an employer and employee, in which the employee agrees not to compete with the employer for a certain period of time after the termination of employment.

Net Promoter Score (NPS): A measure of customer satisfaction and loyalty, calculated by asking customers how likely they are to recommend a product or service to others.

Networking: The process of establishing and maintaining professional relationships for the purpose of exchanging information and opportunities.

New Product Development (NPD): The process of designing, developing, and introducing a new product to the market.

Non-recurring Engineering (NRE): One-time costs associated with the development of a new product, such as research and design expenses.

Negotiations: The process of reaching an agreement between two or more parties by exchanging offers and counteroffers until a mutually acceptable deal is reached.

No-Brainer: A decision or offer that is so clearly advantageous that it requires little or no consideration.

Nootropic: A substance or supplement that enhances cognitive function and performance.

Normalized Earnings Before Interest, Taxes, Depreciation, and Amortization (NEBITDA): A measure of a company's financial performance that excludes the effects of interest, taxes, depreciation, and amortization.

O

Off-Balance Sheet: A financial arrangement in which a company does not include certain assets, liabilities, or obligations on its balance sheet, but instead reports them in the footnotes or other disclosures.

One-Stop Shop: A business or service that provides all the goods or services needed for a particular purpose in one convenient location.

Online Marketplaces: Websites that connect buyers and sellers of goods and services, allowing them to conduct transactions online.

Out-of-Pocket Expenses: The direct and indirect costs of goods or services that are paid for by an individual or business, excluding any insurance or reimbursement.

Outsourcing: The practice of hiring another company or individual to perform services or tasks that are normally done in-house.

Overhead: The indirect or fixed costs of running a business, such as rent, utilities, insurance, and salaries of non-revenue-generating employees.

Operating Expense (OPEX): The cost of running a business, such as salaries, utilities, and office supplies.

Organization Chart: A diagram that shows the structure of a company, including the relationships and relative ranks of its various positions.

Organic Growth: Growth that is achieved through a company's own efforts, rather than through acquisitions or mergers.

Outsourcing: The practice of contracting with an outside firm to perform services or produce goods that are normally performed in-house.

Overhead: The indirect, fixed costs of running a business, such as rent, utilities, and insurance.

Ownership Structure: The way a company is legally organized and owned, including the types and proportions of stock held by various shareholders.

Operations: The processes and activities involved in producing a product or service, including manufacturing, logistics, and customer service.

Option Pool: A reserve of company stock set aside for future grants to employees, executives, and directors.

Online Advertising: Marketing and promotion efforts delivered through the internet, including display ads, search engine marketing, and social media advertising.

Organic Traffic: The volume of visitors to a website that arrive through search engines, as opposed to through paid advertising or other promotional efforts.

P

Parent company: A company that owns and controls one or more subsidiary companies.

Partnership: A business relationship in which two or more individuals or organizations share ownership and profits.

Payroll: The total amount of money paid to employees in a given period, typically a month or a year.

Performance review: An assessment of an employee's job performance, typically conducted on an annual or semi-annual basis.

Permission marketing: A type of marketing that seeks to build customer relationships by providing relevant and valuable information, and seeking consent to communicate with customers.

Pitch deck: A visual presentation used to communicate the key elements of a business plan or investment opportunity.

Platform business: A business model in which a company provides a platform or infrastructure that enables other companies or individuals to sell goods or services.

Point of sale (POS): The location where a customer makes a payment for goods or services, typically at a retail store, restaurant, or other physical location.

Portfolio: A collection of investments held by an individual or organization, typically with the goal of diversifying risk and maximizing returns.

Premium pricing: The practice of charging a higher price for a product or service, due to its perceived value, quality, or scarcity.

Private equity: Investment capital provided to privately-held companies, typically with the goal of acquiring ownership or a significant stake in the company.

Procurement: The process of acquiring goods, services, or materials from suppliers.

Product-market fit: The degree to which a product meets the needs and preferences of its target market.

Professional services: Services provided by professionals, such as lawyers, accountants, or consultants, typically to businesses or other organizations.

Profit margin: The percentage of revenue that remains after all costs have been deducted.

Public relations (PR): The practice of managing the reputation and image of an individual, brand, or organization, through various media channels and tactics.

Public offering: The sale of securities, such as stocks or bonds, to the public, typically through an investment bank or underwriting firm.

Q

Quantitative Research: A research method that involves collecting and analyzing numerical data, often through surveys or experiments.

Queue: A waiting list or line of items to be processed, such as customer orders or support requests.

Quarterly Report: A report issued by a company, typically to its shareholders, that provides an update on its financial performance and outlook for the next quarter.

Quick Wins: Early and relatively easy-to-achieve successes that can build momentum and support for a larger initiative or project.

Quorum: The minimum number of members or participants required to be present for a meeting or decision-making process to proceed.

Quote: An estimate or proposal for the cost of a project, product, or service.

Quality Assurance: The process of verifying that a product or service meets a set of specified quality standards.

Quantum Computing: A type of computing that uses the principles of quantum mechanics to perform certain types of calculations much faster than traditional computers.

Quantitative Analysis: The use of mathematical and statistical methods to analyze and understand data.

Quantitative Easing: A monetary policy used by central banks to increase the money supply and stimulate the economy by purchasing government bonds and other securities.

Quantum Leap: A major advancement or improvement in a particular field or industry.

Quick Win: A small, easily achievable goal or improvement that can have a significant impact in a short amount of time.

Quarterly Report: A report detailing a company's financial performance for a three-month period, typically submitted to regulatory agencies and made publicly available.

R

Revenue: the total amount of money received by a company from its business activities.

Return on Investment (ROI): a financial metric used to measure the return on an investment, expressed as a percentage.

Runway: the length of time a startup has to achieve profitability before it runs out of funding.

Revenue Model: the strategy a company uses to generate revenue, such as selling products or services, advertising, or subscription-based pricing.

Round of Funding: a term used to describe the investment a startup receives from a venture capital firm, angel investor, or other investors.

R&D (Research and Development): Refers to the work a company does in developing new products, services, and technologies.

Rapid Prototyping: A method of quickly creating a physical model of a product idea, to test its viability and functionality.

S

Seed funding: Early stage funding to get a startup off the ground.

Scaling: Increasing the size and reach of a business to increase profitability and growth.

Series A funding: A round of investment that usually follows seed funding and is used to scale the business.

Strategic partnerships: Collaborations between two companies to achieve mutual benefits.

SWOT analysis: An evaluation of a company's strengths, weaknesses, opportunities, and threats.

Sales funnel: A visual representation of the journey a customer goes through to become a buyer.

Start-up - A new business venture usually in the technology or internet-based industries.

Stock options: Options that give employees the right to buy a certain amount of stock at a set price.

Stock options plan: A plan that gives employees the ability to buy shares in the company.

SaaS (Software as a Service): A business model where software is provided on a subscription basis over the internet.

Selling proposition: The unique value a product or service offers to customers.

Service-level agreement (SLA): A formal agreement between a service provider and a customer that defines the level of service.

Start-up incubator: A program that provides support, resources, and mentorship to early-stage startups.

Start-up accelerator: A program that provides mentorship, resources, and funding to early-stage startups.

Strategic plan: A comprehensive plan that outlines a company's goals, strategies, and tactics.

Syndicate: A group of investors who pool their money together to invest in a startup.

Synergy: The added value that results from collaboration between two or more companies.

System integration: The process of connecting different systems to work together seamlessly.

SEO (Search Engine Optimization): The process of optimizing a website to rank higher in search engine results.

Subscription-based model: A business model where customers pay a recurring fee for access to a product or service.

Scalability: The ability of a business or technology to easily handle increased demand and continue to function effectively.

Sales funnel: The process of guiding potential customers through the steps of learning about a product or service, considering a purchase, and making a purchase.

SWOT analysis: A framework for analyzing a company's Strengths, Weaknesses, Opportunities, and Threats.

Systematic risk: The risk that is inherent to an entire market or market segment, rather than a specific company.

Strategic planning: The process of defining a company's goals, resources, and actions to achieve its long-term objectives.

T

Target Market: The specific group of consumers a company aims to sell its products or services to.

Technology Stack: A combination of different software and tools a company uses to develop and run its technology solutions.

Traction: The momentum or growth a startup has gained in its early stages, often measured by metrics such as user acquisition, revenue growth, or media attention.

Target Customer: The ideal customer a company is trying to reach with its products or services.

Technology Roadmap: A plan that outlines the future development of a company's technology products, including the technologies to be used, milestones, and timelines.

Tokenization: The process of converting an asset or liability into a digital token that can be traded and managed on a blockchain network.

Total Addressable Market (TAM): The estimated size of a company's potential market, calculated by multiplying the size of the target market by the market penetration.

Time to Market: The time it takes for a company to bring its product or service to market, from development to commercial launch.

Trade Show: An event where businesses showcase their products or services to potential customers and partners.

Talent Management: The process of attracting, hiring, and retaining employees who have the skills and expertise to help a company achieve its goals.

Total Cost of Ownership (TCO): The total amount spent to acquire and use a product or service, including direct and indirect costs.

Trend Analysis: The process of analyzing trends in sales, customer behavior, or market trends to inform business decisions.

Turnaround Time: The amount of time it takes for a company to recover from a negative situation, such as a decrease in sales or profitability.

Two-Sided Marketplace: A platform that connects buyers and sellers, facilitating transactions between them.

Test Market: A small, controlled market where a company tests the viability of a product or service before launching it in a larger market.

Turnkey Solution: A product or service that is ready to use and requires minimal setup or customization.

Targeted Advertising: Advertising aimed at a specific demographic or market segment.

Technology Transfer: The process of transferring technology from one organization to another, either through licensing, joint ventures, or other means.

Total Quality Management (TQM): A management approach focused on continuously improving all aspects of a company's operations, including products, services, and processes.

U

User Acquisition: The process of attracting and converting users to a product or service.

User Experience (UX): Refers to the overall experience of a user with a product or service, including all aspects of interaction, from usability and design to functionality and content.

User Retention: The percentage of users who continue to use a product or service after their initial acquisition.

Unit Economics: The costs and revenues associated with producing and selling one unit of a product or service.

Upselling: The practice of selling additional or upgraded products or services to existing customers.

User-Generated Content (UGC): Content created by users of a product or service, rather than the company behind it.

Uptime: The amount of time a product or service is operational and available for use.

Unique Visitor: A person who visits a website or uses a product or service for the first time.

Utilization: The amount of a product or service that is used by customers.

Utilization Rate: The percentage of a product or service that is used by customers.

Unique Selling Point (USP): The unique benefit or feature that sets a product or service apart from its competitors.

Upfront Payment: A payment made before delivery of a product or service.

Underlying Technology: The technology that powers a product or service.

User Feedback: Feedback provided by users of a product or service.

User Testing: The process of evaluating a product or service by having users interact with it.

Usability: The ease with which a product or service can be used by its intended users.

Upgrade: An improved version of a product or service.

Unbundled Pricing: A pricing strategy where customers pay separately for each component of a product or service.

Unique Value Proposition (UVP): A statement that clearly communicates the unique benefit a product or service provides to its target market.

User Onboarding: The process of introducing new users to a product or service and helping them get started.

V

Venture Capital: Investment provided by professional investors to startups and growing companies in exchange for an ownership stake.

Valuation: The process of determining the worth or value of a business.

Venture: A high-risk business or investment that seeks to generate substantial returns.

Viral Marketing: A marketing strategy that relies on word of mouth to spread awareness about a product or service.

Virtual Office: An office service provided by a company that allows businesses to have a professional address without a physical office.

Value Proposition: A statement that describes the unique benefits a business offers to its customers.

Virtual Reality: A technology that simulates a real-world environment and allows users to interact with it.

Virtual Assistant: A software or human assistant that provides administrative support and performs tasks remotely.

Volatility: A measure of the amount of uncertainty or risk in the price of a security or asset.

Vertical Integration: A business strategy where a company expands its operations by acquiring or investing in other businesses that operate in the same supply chain.

Venture Debt: Debt financing provided to startups and growth-stage companies that have received venture capital.

Video Marketing: A marketing strategy that uses video content to promote a product or service.

Value Stream Mapping: A visual representation of the process of creating and delivering a product or service.

Value-Based Pricing: A pricing strategy that sets the price of a product or service based on the perceived value it offers to the customer.

Virtual Event: An event that is held online rather than in-person.

Virtual Marketplace: An online platform that allows buyers and sellers to trade goods and services.

Virtual Networking: Networking activities that take place online, such as through social media or video conferencing.

Validation: The process of testing a product or business idea to determine its feasibility and potential for success.

Virtual Reality Headset: A device that allows users to immerse themselves in virtual reality experiences.

Vertical Market: A market that caters to a specific industry or niche, rather than the general population.

W

Workflow - The series of steps or tasks that make up a process.

Webinar - An online seminar or workshop, usually delivered over the internet.

White Label - A product or service that is manufactured by one company and then rebranded by another company for resale.

Wholesale - The sale of goods or products in large quantities at a discounted price.

Wealth Management - The process of providing financial planning, investment management, and other financial services to high-net-worth individuals.

Web Analytics - The measurement, collection, analysis, and reporting of web data for the purpose of understanding and optimizing web usage.

Workforce Management - The planning and management of a company's human resources, including employee scheduling, time and attendance tracking, and payroll processing.

Wearable Technology - A category of electronic devices that are worn on the body, such as smartwatches, fitness trackers, and smart glasses.

Work-Life Balance - The relationship between an individual's work and personal life, and the efforts made to achieve a balance between the two.

Web Development - The process of building, designing, and maintaining websites.

Workplace Diversity - The representation of different perspectives, experiences, and backgrounds in a company's workforce.

Wealth Distribution - The distribution of wealth and assets within a society, often involving the unequal distribution of resources among different groups.

Wireless Technology - Technology that allows for the transfer of data or communication without the use of cables or wires.

Workplace Culture - The shared values, beliefs, attitudes, and behaviors that characterize a company's environment and influence its employees.

Workforce Planning - The process of analyzing and anticipating a company's staffing needs, and making decisions about recruitment, training, and development.

Workplace Safety - The measures taken to ensure the health and safety of employees in the workplace, including the provision of safe working conditions, equipment, and procedures.

Web Hosting - The service of providing storage space and resources for websites, allowing them to be accessible on the internet.

Workforce Training - The process of providing employees with the skills and knowledge necessary to perform their jobs effectively.

Workforce Automation - The use of technology to automate tasks and processes within a company, often resulting in increased efficiency and productivity.

Workforce Diversity - The representation of different backgrounds, experiences, and perspectives within a company's workforce.

X

X-factor: An intangible quality that sets a company or individual apart from others.

X-generation: A term used to describe the next-generation of products, services, or technologies.

X-Marketing: A cross-functional approach to marketing that involves collaboration between different departments within a company.

X-Commerce: The exchange of goods, services, or information over the internet.

X-Functionality: The ability of a product or service to perform multiple functions.

X-Data: Data that is generated by consumers through their digital devices and interactions.

X-Revenue: A type of revenue that comes from a new, unexpected source.

X-Plan: A flexible business plan that can be easily adapted to changing market conditions.

X-Scale: The ability of a company or product to grow and expand quickly.

X-Efficiency: The efficiency of a company or product in using its resources to achieve its goals.

X-Design: A design philosophy that emphasizes user experience, aesthetics, and functionality.

X-Investment: An investment in a company or product with the potential for high returns.

X-Talent: A talented individual or group of individuals with unique skills and abilities.

X-Factor Analysis: A method of analyzing a company or product's potential for success based on its X-factor.

X-Learning: A type of learning that is adaptive and dynamic, constantly changing based on new information and experiences.

X-Innovation: The ability of a company or individual to create new products, services, or technologies.

X-Disrupt: To disrupt an industry or market with a new product, service, or technology.

X-Channels: Multiple channels for distributing and selling a product or service.

X-Price: A flexible pricing strategy that adjusts based on market conditions and customer demand.

X-Organization: A company structure that is agile and adaptive, capable of responding to changing market conditions.

X-Partnership: A partnership between two or more companies that leverages each other's strengths and resources.

X-Communication: A type of communication that is dynamic and adapts to changing circumstances.

X-Technologies: Cutting-edge technologies that are driving innovation and disruption in various industries.

X-Benchmarking: The practice of comparing a company's performance to that of its competitors and industry leaders.

X-Survey: A type of survey that focuses on gathering data and insights on consumer behavior and preferences.

X-Solution: A product or service that solves a specific problem or meets a specific need.

X-Productivity: The efficiency and effectiveness of a company or individual in producing results.

X-Collaboration: A type of collaboration that is flexible and adapts to changing circumstances.

X-Marketing Mix: A combination of marketing strategies and tactics used to promote a product or service.

X-Rebranding: The process of updating and revitalizing a company's brand to remain relevant in a changing market.

Y

Yearly Target - The yearly revenue or sales goal set for a business.

Yellow Pages - A print or online directory of business listings, often sorted by category and area.

Yield Management - The process of adjusting prices for products or services based on supply and demand to maximize profit.

Y Combinator - A startup accelerator that provides seed funding, mentorship, and resources to early-stage startups.

Yottabyte - A unit of digital information storage, equivalent to 1,000 zettabytes or 10^24 bytes.

Year-end Financials - The final financial statements of a business for a given year, including the balance sheet, income statement, and cash flow statement.

YOLO (You Only Live Once) - A catchphrase often used by entrepreneurs to describe the risk-taking attitude they take with their startups.

Yield - The amount of return generated from an investment, expressed as a percentage of the initial investment.

Yellow Belt - A term used in Lean Six Sigma to describe someone who has basic knowledge of the methodology but is not yet certified.

Yarn - A platform for sharing and discovering code packages used by software developers.

Y2K - An abbreviation for "Year 2000", referring to the transition from the 20th to the 21st century and the potential for computer systems to malfunction due to the change in date format.

Year-over-Year (YoY) - A term used to describe the comparison of a metric (such as revenue) between one year and the same period in the previous year.

Yoke - A term used in Agile project management to describe a team structure where two or more teams work together to achieve a common goal.

Yacht Rock - A term used to describe a sub-genre of soft rock music popular in the late 1970s and early 1980s.

Yield Curve - A graph that plots the yield of fixed-income securities against their maturity, used to predict future interest rates.

Yield Strength - The stress at which a material begins to yield, or change shape permanently.

Yellow Journalism - A type of journalism characterized by sensationalism, exaggeration, and a focus on sensational stories, often at the expense of accuracy and ethical journalism practices.

Year-end Bonus - A financial bonus paid to employees at the end of a fiscal year as a reward for their contributions.

Year-to-date (YTD) - A term used to describe the calculation of a metric (such as revenue) from the beginning of the current fiscal year to the present date.

Yoyo Effect - A phenomenon where an individual or organization experiences alternating periods of success and failure.

Z

Zoning: The process of dividing a municipality into areas, or zones, in which specific land uses are permitted or prohibited.

Zero-Based Budgeting (ZBB): A budgeting method where all expenses must be justified for each new period, starting from a "zero base."

Zero-Sum Game: A situation in which one party's gain is equivalent to another party's loss.

Zipcode Targeting: A marketing strategy that focuses on delivering advertising to specific postal code areas.

Zonal Value: The value assigned to a piece of real estate based on its location within a specific zone.

Zone of Influence: An area in which a business or individual has control or significant impact.

Zonal Pricing: A pricing strategy in which products are priced differently based on their geographic location.

Zero-Downtime Deployment: The ability to deploy software updates without interrupting the functioning of a system.

Zonal-Based Data Management: The practice of managing data based on geographic zones or regions.

Zonal Agriculture: An agricultural system that takes into account different soil types, topography, and climates in a specific zone.

Zero-Waste Strategy: A waste management strategy aimed at reducing the amount of waste produced by a business to zero.

Zero-Sum Marketing: A marketing strategy where the goal is to maximize the benefits for the business while minimizing the costs.

Zero-Defects Program: A quality control program that strives for zero defects in the products or services provided.

Zonal Analysis: The process of analyzing data and information based on geographic zones or regions.

Zonal Stacking: A storage strategy where items are stored based on their shipping destination, allowing for more efficient picking and packing processes.

Zonal Management System: A system used to manage resources and operations within a specific geographic zone.

Zonal Development Plan: A plan outlining the development goals and objectives for a specific geographic zone.

Zonal Reporting: The practice of reporting on the performance of a business based on geographic zones or regions.

Zero-Liability Policy: A policy offering protection for consumers against unauthorized transactions on their bank accounts or credit cards.

Zero-Cost Marketing: Marketing tactics that do not incur any direct cost, such as word-of-mouth marketing or viral marketing.

CONCLUSION

In conclusion, "The Corporate Language: Navigating the Terminology of the Startup World" has provided a comprehensive overview of the key terms used in the world of startups. This guide has been designed to help founders, investors, and aspiring entrepreneurs understand the language of business and succeed in the competitive world of startups.

If you have found this book to be useful, please share it with others who may benefit from it. Your support and feedback are greatly appreciated.

I hope this book serves as a valuable resource on your journey to success in the world of startups. Thank you for choosing "The Corporate Language" as your guide to the terminology of the startup world.

Rohan Shaw

9 798889 599982

Printed by Libri Plureos GmbH in Hamburg, Germany